FIRST NATIONS MONOLOGUES

edited by
JANE HARRISON

CURRENCY PRESS
The performing arts publisher

First published in 2023
by Currency Press Pty Ltd,
Gadigal Land, PO Box 2287, Strawberry Hills, NSW, 2012, Australia
enquiries@currency.com.au
www.currency.com.au

Cover design by Laura La Rosa for Currency Press.
Currency Press acknowledges the Traditional Owners of the Country on which we live and work. We pay our respects to all Aboriginal and Torres Strait Islander Elders, past and present.

A catalogue record for this book is available from the National Library of Australia

CONTENTS

INTRODUCTION

This anthology was edited on Wadawurrung Land and produced on Gadigal Land. This country was never ceded.

Wherever it appears in the script—the intriguing opening, in the middle as a turning point, or at the end as a denouement or summing up of the journey of the play—a good monologue captures the attention. It is a spilling out of all that character is feeling, and it has the emotional expressiveness of a punch.

A monologue has the actor alone, physically or metaphorically, in the spotlight, and directing the speech towards the silent listener —to the audience, an offstage character, a departed character or, if an interior monologue, simply to themselves. The monologue is the stalwart of the actors' audition process and it needs to demonstrate the range of what the actor can do. Brutal, charming, poetic or reflective, or all of the above in turns, a good monologue is an opportunity for the actor to strut their stuff, to seduce their audience with a direct address.

For First Nations actors, finding a suitable monologue has been challenging up to now. But in recent times, with so many First Nations plays having been published and performed, the challenge was what to leave out of this anthology. The First Nations-authored plays from which these monologues have been selected, be they comedies, dramas or biographical plays, have played in our leading theatres and have often smashed box office receipts. But more importantly they have contributed to a body of work where the First Nations voice and lived experience has been privileged in an act of decolonisation. Peterson declares that First Nations' dramatic monologues are 'a vehicle for playwrights to literally write themselves into the land with great cultural specificity'.

So many of these First Nations Monologues deal with the big topics in life—death: the aftermath and grief of it (*Barbara and the Camp Dogs*); investigating deaths in custody (*Into the Bigness*); suicide (*Brothers Wreck*); the funeral as a celebration of a life (*Tiddas*).

The love of country is another strong theme, evident in the monologues (*The Visitors, Sunshine Super Girl*). Justice and the need for self-determination also are abiding themes (*At What Cost?*).

Some of these monologues have a lighter touch, displaying the Blak humour Blak plays are renowned for, including takes on that stock-in-trade of the playwrighting genre, the dysfunctional family (*Cursed!*) but even the so-called functional family (*Black is the New White*) allows for humour and self-deprecation.

These excerpts represent writing that is *for* First Nations communities and audiences first. Writing *for* and *with*, rather than 'about', as so many non-First Nations-authored plays with blackfella themes or storylines do.

For those who are students of the playwrights' craft, these monologues will also serve, giving us the finely honed single story. We hope this collection sparks your interest in First Nations-authored plays and gives an insight into their variety, depth and scope. The monologue is a powerful beast.

Jane Harrison, 2023

JADA ALBERTS

Brothers Wreck

Brothers Wreck *tells the story of a young Black man, Ruben, in the aftermath of his cousin's suicide. Dealing with guilt, grief and regret, but also strength and the power of connection,* Brothers Wreck *takes the audience on a rollercoaster ride of emotions, raw and visceral.*

In this excerpt, Ruben recounts the discovery of his cousin's body and his despair at the thought that he might have been able to intervene in time to save him.

Ruben

I wanted to learn how to throw, remember? I woulda been happy to just keep chuckin the bastard till I knocked the fish out, but I knew I could learn. I wanted to do something good. I wanted us to be the best fishermen the harbour had ever seen, I wanted to live like my grandfathers' lived, I wanted to know what it felt like to be proud of myself. So I bought the net. I bought the net. [*Beat.*] We drank in the driveway till four, it was about four I think, I fell asleep in the chair. I woke up 'cause, 'cause you changed the music. I yelled at you to turn it down. I think it was four. [*Beat.*] I came inside, I felt sick. I had to sleep. I, I crashed on the couch. [*Beat.*] I was gone, out of it, till you shook me. You shook me awake. 'Ruben, wake up, man, come look at this.' [*Beat.*] I was heavy, I couldn't, I couldn't. [*Beat.*] 'Fuck off, Joe, I've had enough, let me sleep.' [*Beat.*] 'Let me sleep,' I said.

Pause.

You let me sleep. [*Beat.*] I woke. I thought I heard mice, scampering, scratching, frantic. [*Beat.*] Then it stopped.

Pause.

I lay awake, wondering what it was. By the time I got outside it was too late. You'd stopped moving. I saw the net, the sinkers scraping, all wrapped around, your feet just touching the bottom of the pipe. It wasn't mice, it was you. [*Beat.*] Lift him up! Lift him up! Lift him up! [*Beat.*] Too late. [*Beat.*] You're gone. [*Beat.*] I should've got up. You asked me to get up. Fuck! Why didn't I get up?!

Pause.

No matter what, you always had time for me. No matter what, you were always there for me. [*Beat.*] I won't ever be the same, Joe. I…

Pause.

I sat there. I couldn't move. [*He can't help but cry.*] I tried to tell Del, I did, when she woke up I tried to say something before she saw you, nothing came out. I was stuck, and they found you and I couldn't move, I couldn't move, I don't know what happened, I couldn't move. I'm so sorry, I should've got up, I should've helped get you down, I was stuck. I couldn't move! That whole time I couldn't move, I tried, I did, that whole day I prayed that I'd move, please let me fucking move!

HENRIETTA BAIRD

The Weekend

The Weekend *encapsulates one woman's crazy night trying to find her partner, Simon, who has left their kids at home unsupervised. Lara follows a trail of clues that takes her to the Housing Commission towers, confronting drug dealers and druggies. There she meets the dealer Ronnie, who tries to help Lara, in her own deluded way.*

In this scene, Ronnie tells Lara about how her kids were removed from her.

Ronnie

I need a break.

I hate this park, I haven't been down here for ages.

This is where DoCS took my kids.

I left my kids with my sister DD while I met a client down at the Cross. I taught DD everything she knows about selling.

She brung the kids here so she could meet with Betty and a new customer. She learnt the hard way. Don't trust outsiders!

I came back to meet DD and pick up the kids. I sat on this swing and waited and waited, it felt like ages sis. Then Betty comes running up to me and tells me that DD was in the lock up and DoCS had taken my kids. The new guy was a fucken nark.

Fuckin DD got my kids taken off me! My own sister, I raised her up after our mum hung herself and she couldn't even keep my kids safe for one day. I haven't had anything to do with her since then. I tried to get my kids back but nothing. DoCS made it clear to me that I was an unfit Mother. What would they know about being an unfit mother? They didn't see what DD and I went through with our mum.

Ah fuck em anyways. Speaking of the cheeky bitch...

Come on then, let's go see that fresh fork sister of mine ...

The following is the last scene in The Weekend. *Lara has learned the cold hard truth about her addicted partner and has decided to cut her losses. The weekend's over and she's returned to Cairns, where she's rehearsing a dance performance.*

Lara

Flights booked and I think fuukkk!

I could've lost my boys last night. I could have been Ronnie. I could of got busted and my boys could've been taken by DoCS. For once in my life, someone was looking out for me. I was meant to meet Ronnie, DD, Courtney and Betty because I realised then I'm an addict like them. I'm an addict of love, jealousy, and abuse, and Simon was how I got my fix. This time I'm quitting cold turkey. No more chances.

I get back to work I look into the Clean Studio mirrors and I see myself. I'm tired, my body is sore, muscles are aching and my heart is broken, but I'm alive, and my kids are safe. Just before it's my turn to dance across the floor one of the other dancers ask me, Sis, how was your weekend?

Oh you know, I just chassayed, partaborayed step step, pirouette, step step, and jette all weekend.

KODIE BEDFORD

Cursed!

Everything is complicated and a little crazy in Bernadette's family, but it makes for great comic material. Because if you didn't laugh … With lashings of religious guilt, siblings coming out, and a white Nan on her deathbed, Cursed! *takes on themes of intergenerational mental illness. What do you inherit from your family, and what can you avoid inheriting with the right intervention and intentions?*

In this scene, Bernadette gives her therapist a glimpse into her complex family dynamic with a mad mum.

Bernadette

I've never been to therapy before. I know what you'll say. Blame my childhood. Isn't that what they say? That's the prime time for fast-tracking fuck-ups. But I can tell you right now it wasn't my childhood … I mean, sure, my earliest memories are visiting my mother in a mental institution but I can say with confidence that my childhood was completely normal … Apart from the mental institution bit. There are many adult reasons why a person can be depressed. Mortgage stress for example. I don't have a mortgage but if I had one, particularly here in Sydney, I would be very depressed. And I don't have any prospects of buying a house because both of my parents live in public housing and I have no equity to borrow off.

It's a relief really. So I guess my point is that I'm not depressed about mortgages and I really don't know why I had a breakdown at Louisa's Hawaiian themed thirtieth birthday party in Surry Hills. It just came upon me. We could be talking about anything; all the pressures of modern day life. Climate change. Politics. Catholics. I'm not Catholic but I was raised as a Catholic and went to Catholic school. I wasn't molested or anything. Sorry, when you say to people you went to a Catholic school, you immediately have to assure them you weren't touched. And if you were, that's a conversation stopper. Not that there's anything wrong with that. I mean there *is* something wrong with that. Shit. I'm sorry. Is that what I need to talk about in these sessions? Catholics? The non-touched variety of Catholics. Nan who raised us was as devout as they came. I'm talking rosary every night with my brother and sister. Praying for people—alcoholics, heathens, racists, Great Aunt Mildred who ticks all three boxes. But come to think of it, I don't think being a Catholic made me depressed. And it wasn't my childhood. Nan gave us a loving, sane, safe, somewhat Catholic (non-touched) childhood! Good country living. Geraldton in the Midwest of Western Australian. Yeah no-one has heard of it. But it is famous for the Batavia massacre, rape and pillaging. [*Smiling*] I miss it. [*Realising*] Not the massacre or rape or pillaging. I just miss the place. It may be a little more conservative but it's simple. People over here in the east complicate shit. Even racism is complicated— you have 'institutional racism', 'lateral violence', 'micro aggression'... sometimes I just miss the WA simplicity of being called a black cunt. Simplicity is good for me.

WESLEY ENOCH

Black Medea

Wesley Enoch has created a rich and poetic adaptation of the classic Greek play,
Medea, *interweaving threads of Indigenous storytelling within the framework of
the ancient Greek myth.*

*In his version Medea, a young Indigenous woman finds herself displaced from
her homeland and in a loveless marriage to the drunk and violent Jason. The
script touches on a taboo topic—infanticide—but asks us to see the story, though
steeped in Indigeneity, as a universal one.*

*In this scene, Medea calls out to the ancestral spirits, appearing to her in the
shape of the wind.*

Medea

I am not frightened of you. I have faced everything I fear and
defeated it. You think you are a match for me? The day has finally
come... and today... I will vanquish you. Today... Jason and I will
no longer run. And you will feel the sharpened edge of a mother's
love and a wife's loyalty.

I can feel you, I can hear you coming. I am ready for you. Hear me...
I am ready for you.

Come out and face me. Face me!

This is not a fit place for our final battle. But here you have chosen and here it must be. Were it up to me I would choose the open desert where you could not hide amongst these scared strangers clutching to the coast like cowering children.

I have not sacrificed everything to fail now. I have dreams.

Who am I to have such dreams? Who am I to go against even you?

I am a daughter of this Land, I have the knowledge of my people. I have the power of my clan, I have the strength of my marriage, I have the love of my husband, I have the weapons of my wits. I am Medea.

So come now and face me.

There is a blood debt to pay and not a drop of mine shall fall upon the thirsty earth.

The Story of the Miracles at Cookie's Table

The Story of the Miracles at Cookie's Table *is a multigenerational tale. A birth tree is cut down and becomes a table in a white man's house, with the Black woman a maid serving at that table. Years later the table returns to Black ownership but who can claim it? Mother and son fight for the table and the many layered stories of family life around the table are shared and contested.*

In this scene, the mother, Annie, directs her straight talking at her son, with whom she's not that impressed.

Annie

Fuck off, I said! [*Pause.*] You go on about black this and black that—I'm your elder smart arse/ you want to be black you start showing me some respect. You come here with your big words… thinking to run rings around me with your university bullshit. You can't choose your family. There's a bit of wisdom for you, prick. I'm still your mother whether you like it or not. And she was my mother whether I liked it or not, and I never bad-mouthed my mother to her face like you do. I showed her respect. You know what family is? Do you? Growing up here all sheltered—it's full of secrets/ and lies/ and we all—every one of us/ we'd rather tell those stories from long ago than tell each other the truth from today/ now/ here. You know what family is? It's not blood/ fucken most of the island's got the same blood, but I wouldn't call half them arseholes my family—family is respect. When that's gone, then no use calling yourself black no more. There'll be no blackfellas left when that's gone… You want to feel what it's like having no family/

do ya?/ You walk with me through this place and watch your own blood turn away from you—can't look you in the eye… that's not respect, that's not family. No wonder this place is falling apart [*yelling*] everyone's got their heads so far up their arse they don't know what sunshine is no more!

In this next scene Annie speaks to her mother Faith about how her Uncle betrayed her when she was thirteen.

Annie

You never believed me. I was some slut/ some whore who turned her back on God. You were gone to a church meeting on the mainland. I kicked up such a stink, you said you'd pray for my soul. And it rained and the lightning/ like the sky was ripping apart, like a war was happening. Like the devil himself was being cast out of heaven. And he was—he came in the shape of a man soaked, in black, and he held me down and I said that prayer—Our father who art in heaven/ He took off his wet clothes, he said they needed to dry—He told me I was pretty. No-one had called me pretty before. And then he grabbed my arm and pulled me close to him/ He held me against his wet black skin and he smelt… of stale piss and cigarettes. He told me I was pretty and he kissed me on my bare neck, he grabbed my hair and he touched me. My own uncle… I was thirteen. He called me pretty and then he called me a slut. He took my innocence. They must have heard me scream, they must have heard me call out but no-one came—no-one came to help.

A crack of thunder and the lights of the house go out. ANNIE *and* FAITH *are dimly lit.*

I was thirteen. You were meant to look after me. You were meant to believe me. I have not got a dirty soul… I have not got a dirty soul…

RICHARD FRANKLAND

Conversations with the Dead

Jack investigates Aboriginal deaths in custody and is haunted by those stories and the family members he speaks to about the loss of their loved ones in prison.

In this scene, Jack speaks about his anger, and how it manifests in violence, and his grief at the lives, and deaths, he is forced to investigate.

Jack

have hurt people. I smashed people in bars. I smashed people in the street. I intimidated people, I scared myself. I was alone in my anger and in my fear. I got to see how cruel they could be, how we were nothing in their eyes, victims, subhuman.

Look at him sitting there on the morgue table. Look at him.

You know what? I wish me and him were in the bush, maybe by the sea. I wish he was alive and we could have tied knots together, fished maybe, drunk beer and laughed, told bullshit stories 'bout our families and lives.

Even now, even now I say to people, you should see what I've seen, you should see what I see in my mind. I learnt to read between the lines, I say.

I'm scared, I say.

Scared that if I open my mouth to start screaming I won't stop. That I'll scream until I die, until I'm empty and there is nothing left inside of me. I'm scared that I'll scream so loud it will change the world. Or that no-one will hear it at all or if they do no-one will care.

Walking into the Bigness

This autobiographical play touches on moments in the incredible life of Richard Frankland, from his relationship with his mother, his time in the Army and on fishing boats, and his role investigating Aboriginal deaths in custody.

In this scene, Richard is applying for a role with the Aboriginal Legal Service, and he points out the burdens of the role.

Richard

I t's the mid-80s. *Crocodile Dundee 2*—the one with Ernie Dingo as the blackfella. And I won't take the dole. No way. Chaos juggling work, feeding the family, people coming and going—

Get a job interview. So I go down to the dole office and say:

Can I borrow some money? I don't want a dole cheque, I just want some money for petrol. I'll pay it back.

Get the money and, ah, get the job.

Aboriginal Legal Service. You have to pay a third of your own petrol and a third of your own phone bill. And you are on call twenty-four-seven for the whole state, but they pay you two hundred and something dollars a week.

Then investigator/field officer, get appointed to Royal Commission into Black Deaths in Custody, 1988. Ha! Tall ships. Bicentenary. Fireworks. And it's probably the worst job I ever done in my life. For a long time I was the only Indigenous employee for some two and a half states. The first wage they offer me was eighteen thousand dollars per annum. The second was twenty-eight thousand. I receive no training. My role is to locate witnesses, take statements from both black and white people, and to talk to other interested parties of the Commission's proceedings.

And sometimes you wear a suit, because it's a voice game now, and who's got the most power. And they're all scared—cops and screws— of a Royal Commission. So you walk down a hallway [*clicking his fingers*] and there's three or four governors, there's all these guards, all around you, and you stop. [*He stops clicking.*]

And you adjust your suit. And you start walking again. [*Clicking his fingers*] You show them you've got the power.

And you get into that room with that woman, and you throw them all out, and you are holding her in your arms, she's crying, there's fifty stitches in her throat and another fifty or so in each arm, and all the time you've got no power to get her out; and a clear fluid from her body leaks down into your suit, and you drive home and you have to have a shower with your suit on because the fluid has stuck the suit to your body.

Ninety-nine deaths investigated, sixty in police custody. I work on a huge mob of them. Seven in detail: three were elders, one had a young family, three were stolen generation, one was an adolescent, one they beat so hard his heart was lying on his spine.

In this scene a teenage Richard has left Broome with his Mother, and they are hitching their way across the country.

Richard

We're about three thousand k's in. Me and Mum.

Yeah, I'd gone back home. Now I'm outside of a town on the Nullarbor somewhere, hungry, walking—been up to Broome for my sister's wedding, hitchhiked to Perth, slept under a tree at the Kalgoorlie turn-off. We'd lost our house in Portland, but most of the family's in Canberra so we're heading there. Things hadn't turned out so we'd left Broome with no money. Not a zac, not a brass razoo. I am the man. I am fifteen. It's 1979. We walk and walk and walk.

Here the land seems to go on forever. And I, I've lost everything. Got nothing. Can't even get a feed. No money. No blankets. And I am not sure why, but—I have this canvas bag full of my songs, poems, stories. And so I, I just walk into the bigness—Mum's watching—and I pull it all out and throw it as hard as I can.

From nowhere a willy-willy comes and picks it up mid-flight and grabs it all and whizzes it around. Mum yells, 'No!' and runs into the willy-willy.

Her hair's flinging about, whipped up, down, to the side. She's yelling and snatching it all back from the wind. It was like she was challenging nature itself. And she snatches the stuff, the songs, the poems, and the rest.

I am breathless, watching. The willy-willy passes, off into the distance, a whirl of dust, fearless in its journey. Mum stands there, tears falling, hair everywhere, handfuls of my writings. Without a word I take them from her and stuff them back in my bag. Dunno what else to do with 'em. Decide that I gotta keep writing though. Gotta get out of here first and find myself another job.

JANE HARRISON

Stolen

This play centres on the experiences and confusion, grief and longing of five children who were removed from family as part of the government-sanctioned Stolen Generations. It plays with time and place and focuses on vignettes from their lives.

In this scene, Sandy, who was removed at an older age and retains some of his traditional storytelling customs, tells the bittersweet story of how he was named, and his mother's unstinting love for him despite what she went through.

Sandy

My people are from the desert. Home of the red sands. When I was a little boy, my mother would tell me the story of how the desert sands were created, a long time ago. Our people were very vain. Neighbouring mob were coming over for a visit and my ancestors wanted our land to look better than anyone else's. The boss man said, 'We will build a special meeting place circled by big red rocks, the biggest rocks we can find.'

The chorus become the big red rocks.

So the men searched and found these big red rocks and they rolled them into a big circle. When the neighbouring nation came over they said, 'Very magic spot.' But then banga—the Old Wind— [*Aside to* JIMMY] Jimmy, you be banga—The Old Wind high up in the sky was blowing by and he saw what my people had done to fool their neighbours and he laughed and laughed at them. He laughed and he roared around the rocks and they all crumbled into sand and blew all over, until the land, he was covered in red sand.

The others act out being the whirling, swirling sand, until they spin slowly back in the direction of their beds.

That's how the desert sands were created. My mum used to laugh 'n laugh at that story. She was always laughing, my old mum. Had a sense of humour.

The kids creep back into their beds and SANDY *is left to finish his story alone.*

She used to say that when you walk on the sand, the wind can blow away your footsteps, like you had never made them, and the earth would become pure again. The sand could heal itself. The land where my people come from is covered in red sand and in the old days, the women, to try and stop the white men from raping them, would shove sand inside themselves. Anything to stop the men from raping them, anything. [*He becomes quieter.*] And that's what my mother did, but it didn't stop them and so I came along. My mother, she loved me, but she called me Sandy anyway. She sure had a sense of humour, that one.

Rainbow's End

Rainbow's End *is set in the 1950s and tells the story of three generations of Aboriginal women living on 'the flats', a flood-prone area on the edge of town in regional Victoria. The play captures their struggles to put food on the table, get a roof over their heads, and secure a good job for the youngest, Dolly.*

In this scene, towards the end of the play, Dolly's mother Gladys, who has only just learnt to read, bravely gets up in a public meeting to deliver a petition protesting her community's living conditions.

Gladys

Your Majesty, Queen Elizabeth the Second. We demand suitable housing for the Aboriginal people. [*To herself*] Yes, we got Rumbalara. And I'll be the first to admit, the idea sounded good. But—have you seen it? Concrete. No doors inside—so, we don't need privacy, not like regular folk, is that it? We want decent houses. Mrs Windsor, would you live at Rumbalara? Then why is it good enough for us? Why do we have to prove we can live like whitefellas, before we get the same opportunities? And, to boot, we're watched over like a bunch of cheeky kids … We're second class citizens in our own country. No, we're not even citizens. Heavens, and this is the 50's!

We *demand* the right to control our own destiny. Now how exactly did Papa Dear word it?

She looks at the paper. She's lost her train of thought. She begins to panic.

She looks at the piece of paper wildly. There is a sustained moment of tension, then she hesitatingly reads one word, then another, then another.

We demand the right to make our own decisions, and not be at the whim of Government, at the mercy of Protection Boards, at the vagary of Landlords and property owners.

We demand proper schooling. [*To herself*] And not just for us. The white people too - they need to be educated about us, and our ways.

She is reading more fluently now.

Opportunities. We want jobs in town for our sons and daughters. We want them to go to Universities. [*To herself*] Yes! Not just high schools but Universities! And why not? They say we can't learn, but we can. We can do anything once we set our minds to it, eh?

We, the undersigned, demand to be the equal of anyone. And we will fight for that right. And keep fighting. Until we are treated right. By our neighbours and employers. By the Shire, by the Crown, by Mr Menzies. [*To herself*] And if it's not him, then the next Prime Minister. Or the one after that.

Lastly, and this isn't in the petition, but maybe it should be, I don't want my mother to be served last in the butchers. And I want townsfolk to say 'hello, lovely day'. Not cross the road to avoid us like we're lepers. [*To her audience*] We can get along with each other, can't we?

The Visitors

This play tells of the arrival of the First Fleet in 1788, but entirely from the perspective of seven Elders on the shore of Warrane, who must decide whether to send these strangers away or allow them to land.

This scene comes at the end of the play. Gordon, on whose country the First Fleet are poised to land, must overcome his hatred of the strangers and what they represent, and finish what his own father began 18 years before, which is to deliver a welcome to country. He addresses the boats.

Gordon

This is my country.

My father's country.

I know its patterns, its seasons, its soils, the texture of them, the colours, the particular shade of green of the grass the patyegarang nibbles after a fire has swept through, at dusk, when the patyegarang is most hungry, and most likely to be speared.

I know its secret springs where a thirst can be quenched even in the driest season.

I know my country's smells. The exact scent of leaf litter where bulbs of the chocolate lily hide under moss, though it is not my job to collect them.

And where the hardest flint is to be found. For tools, for trading.

Its rivers are my blood, its rocky outcrops my bones, its winds are my breath as my lungs fill and empty. It is me.

When I welcome others, I honour my country.

We ask this, and this only.

While you walk on this country that you care for the land.

And that you look after the children of this land.

This is my country and my son's country.

In honour of my father, I welcome you to country.

ANITA HEISS

Tiddas

Tiddas *tells the story of five women and their enduring friendship from their time growing up in Mudgee, to their present lives in Brisbane. They meet regularly to discuss Blak literature at their bookclubs. Each of the women is dealing with their own issues—trying to get pregnant, becoming unexpectedly pregnant, dating, battling an alcohol dependency, battling loneliness after a divorce. But they have each other's backs—mostly.*

In this scene Ellen, the Blak celebrant, delivers the eulogy for her Aunt back in Mudgee.

Ellen

Aunty Molly and Uncle Ron were married for almost fifty years. She was the love of his life. He tells me that a cup of tea on the veranda and morning walks along the Cudgegong River at Lawson Park is all they needed. Quiet times together were more important than the trips to the big city. They had all the romance they needed right here in Mudgee, with each other. From the day Aunt put that wedding ring on his hand, Uncle has never taken it off. 'They'll have to pry it from my cold dead hands', he used to say, but Aunty Molly didn't like Uncle quoting Charlton Heston, even as a joke. Still, she always laughed at his jokes, that unconditional love kind of laugh you give because the person in front of you fills your heart completely. Aunty Molly was sunshine and rainbows and the sound of singing nightingales rolled into one.

Ellen *chokes up*.

And she was Uncle Ron's Koori Rose.

ANDREA JAMES

Winyanboga Yurringa

Six contemporary Aboriginal women gather on country and through their inter-actions questions of kinship, belonging and responsibility are hashed out. The fair-skinned Jadah has to come to terms with how she fits into community and whether she is accepted—or not.

In this scene, Jadah ruminates on the dichotomy within her, her blackness masked by her white skin, and how that makes her feel.

JADAH *strips off her clothes to her singlet and undies and takes a long deep dive into the river. She floats and lets the current take her away.*

Jadah

Whiteness exposed
My blackness flails about
One punches the other
I am bruised
Inside and out
She's not my enemy
The enemy is within
Family trees
Branches lopped off

Blood spurts

This way and that

This is pure horror

I hate you

This black and this white

Within

This oil and this water

Cancelling me out

In equal measure

This is me

Claim me

Take me

Bleed me

This is me

I know this to be true

I am my father's daughter

From the freshwater

I am my grandmother's daughter

From the mountains, to the lakes, to the sea

I know this to be true

I am me

This here

This place here

Is me.

Yanagai! Yanagai!

Yanagai! Yanagai! *re-imagines the fight of the Yorta Yorta people in the 1980s to claim their land rights in an historic legal trial. In real life, the Yorta Yorta were denied their claim, with the judge telling them their connection had been 'washed away by the tides of history'. James' play has a different outcome, one that fiercely demonstrates the enduring connection to country of the Yorta Yorta people.*

In this scene, Munarra, a Yorta Yorta superhero, rejects the court process and reaffirms their sovereignty.

Munarra

As long as this river flows, the lake fills and floods, the redgums sway and grow—we are here. For as long as the eagle flies and the long-neck turtle swims—we are here. Like every grain of sand on our river's shores—we are here. Like the line that connects me to my traditions—we are here. Like every leaf on every branch on every tree on this land—we are here. We are here! We are here!

> *The* MEN *stop shovelling and fade out of existence. They shed their Driza-Bones and join* MUNARRA *in a line of defiance. A war stance.*

And I am not your judgement. I am not your 'Exhibit A'.

I am not your servant.

I am Yorta Yorta.

We are Yorta Yorta.

And…

WE… ARE… HERE.

Sunshine Super Girl

This uplifting and exhilarating play tells the story of champion tennis player Evonne Goolagong Crawley's development as a player from a small kid hitting a found ball against the shed, to the courts of the biggest, most prestigious competitions in the world.

In this scene, Evonne has slipped back into her country hometown and has found a quiet place to fish and reminisce.

Evonne

This is a good spot here. This is Mum's spot.

That current there? Swirling around and around? That's the backwater. Leaves and twigs and bugs. That's what the fish are after and that's what I'm after.

The fish.

My dad told me about the magic of fishing at the backwater.

He used to say, 'See that big hole down there? Plenty of fish. Big ones. That's where you go to catch a fish.'

But to tell you the truth, if I don't catch a fish, that's okay too … No-one knows I'm here. Not even family. I'm not ready to go into town. Just yet.

Yesterday I fished around the corner. A bit closer to the bend and I caught three fish! Yellow belly and cod.

One pan size, one baking dish size and one family size.

Caught 'em on some worms. Took me two hours.

She smells her fingers.
Still got that fishy smell. It's starting to sink in.

Look out!

A fish bites. She scrambles to hook it, but misses.
Missed him!

Freshwater woman, through and through.

When I throw in a line and I'm waiting for a bite, it's like I'm on the court.

In the zone.

Your hearing changes—like you're underwater.

Your muscles shift and tighten. Ready for anything.

Your vision is sharp. Every twitch, every flutter.

And when everything aligns, that ball moves in slow motion and comes up to meet you.

Like an old friend.

And when you hit that sweet spot:

'Toc'!

It's like pure heaven.

That ball flies like a bird.

You watch your opponent scramble and before she hits the ball. Wham!

You're there. You know where to be.

She winds in her line, gets down from the umpire's chair, walks to the centre of the court and picks up a handful of Wiradjuri dirt.

But why did I win, when so many others have lost? What did it cost?

Why me?

Dogged

This clever play uses the dingo, whose mate was shot and whose puppies disappeared, as a metaphor for the effects of the Stolen Generations.

In this scene, Dingo talks to Dog, who has begun to hang around with Dingo, about being hunted down. The following monologue is by Andrea James, from the play cowritten with Catherine Ryan.

Dingo

t's no bloody holiday here, mate.

This place is dangerous.

The other day, I was looking for a feed

with my pack.

Mum, Dad and the kids.

Beyond the piss marks,

comfort zone gone.

But we were starving.

Looking for food

anything will do.

And I'm tracking a lizard under the stones, my mate has got his eyes on a skinny looking rabbit and the little ones are pouncing on grasshoppers.

Yum yum yum.

And then it starts.

Bang!

They've got their sights on us.

Upwind.

I didn't smell a fucking thing.

Bang!

Mate for life goes down.

Noooooo!

And I yell to the little ones …

Run!

Bang!

And we run!

Through the long grass.

In between the rocks.

Bang!

Sparks fly

and I yell to the little ones …

Run!

Around the trees

and up that cliff there …

Run!

My paws grab the rocks and I'm climbing,

cliff hanging!

Up and up and up and up!

Bang!

I pull myself up and over and look down …

Pause.

My mate lying there.

Blood pouring out of his ears and mouth.

No little ones.

Nothing. Just a smattering of blood on the sunlit rock.
A scuff.

There's a gunshot in the distance. DINGO *pricks her ears.*
Have you seen my little ones?

NAKKIAH LUI

Black is the New White

Charlotte is a Black lawyer, the shining hope of her family. But she's in love with Francis, a white experimental composer, who is also the son of her father's political enemy. How do you resolve love, and Christmas, when your families have other ideas?

In this scene the political positions of the two patriarchs are laid out.

Narrator

The antagonism between Ray Gibson and Dennison Smith was never perceived by others as a great rivalry it was in their own minds.

They were political opponents during the naughty nineties when Australian politics was on the brink of great social change the landscape was dotted with ideological egos. Ray Gibson was the handsome, charismatic Aboriginal politician with a great head of hair, who was at one point being touted as the future leave leader of the Labor Party. Dennison Smith was a dour, conservative social services minister for the Liberal Party who wore very expensive suits and had ambitions for the prime ministership that were supported by no one.

Neither can quite remember the exact moment when they became enemies, but their rivalry peaked when Ray threw his shoe across the floor at Dennison. Dennison tried to have Ray thrown out of parliament but no one cared.

Throughout the husbands' tumultuous years as political rivals, Marie and Joan managed to maintain civil acquaintance mainly thanks to the enthusiasm of Marie, who was always very, very, very fond of Joan. Marie Smith has recently come to a very big revelation about herself that she is yet to reveal to anyone. Especially Dennison. She plans to tell him on New Year's Eve. After this Christmas. The first they have spent with their son, Francis, in six years ... That's 19.2 Aboriginal years.

Blaque Showgirls

Identity politics gets a satirical workout in Blaque Showgirls, *where wannabe blackfella, Ginny, travels to BrisVegas to audition for Blaque Showgirls, the worlds best cultural and sexually authentic dance revue, meeting up with Molly, a young Aboriginal girl who has claimed her Irish heritage.*

In this scene Molly spells out her reasons for turning her (black) back on her Aboriginal heritage.

Molly

Ginny, I know it's your dream to be a Blaque Showgirl but being a Blaque Showgirl means you're Aboriginal and being Aboriginal in this country isn't a good thing, you should know that!

I hated always being followed around stores by security. Not being able to get a taxi or my Uber rating always being low even though I was always quiet and polite and never slammed the door!

Not getting approved for rentals. Or getting pulled over by police—even when I was just standing!

Always nervous when anything to do with Aboriginal people was brought up in case it was racist.

Not being able to watch morning TV in case there was a panel on 'Aboriginal dysfunction'. People always thinking I got free stuff or special treatment just because I was Aboriginal.

My family constantly suffering and dying from chronic health issues.

Kids being stolen.

Living in constant fear.

Never feeling safe.

Generation after generation of having no worth as person in this country.

Aboriginal people die eight years before non-Aboriginal people and I didn't just want live longer, I wanted to live!

Live a life where I wasn't defined first and foremost by my race.

No-one ever saw 'Alinta'. They just saw an Aboriginal woman.

One day, when looking at a missing poster, I realised that white women get to be seen as individuals! When white women go missing or get murdered, they get called by their names and get their own posters! Alone!

Black women ... it's always 'Aboriginal' first even if anyone notices or they just wait until enough of us die and then there's a march or hashtag and then ... nothing.

When white women are angry, it's a reckoning. They get books and speaking tours!

When I was angry, I was a problem to be destroyed or worse ... ignored.

And I was so so angry. So angry I couldn't just be the person I wanted to be. That being Aboriginal determined my value in every aspect of my life and I had no say in it!

None at all!

So being white ... wow ... it seemed incredible. So when I discovered I was white it was like a weight lifted off my shoulders. I mean, look at confirmations—white people don't need them! So I tore mine up and I decided I wasn't going to suffer anymore. I was going to embrace my heritage, take my privilege and be white!

In this scene the star and icon of the show, Chandon, describes what being a Blaque Showgirl means.

Chandon

Blaque Showgirls was created for Blaque women, every Blaque Woman, to come and be celebrated in a world that refuses to see them as people.

Black Women who are the scariest threats because we can never be a white man, not even close.

Black Women whose success is deemed as a threat.

Black Women whose labour is expected but never considered success.

Black Women whose voices are deemed less or too disruptive to have worth.

Black women who are either Aunty or Gins, Sluts or Victims, Angry or Silent, invisible or targeted, excellent or villified.

Black Women who aren't included in Black or white history.

Black Women whose self empowerment is seen as radical because how dare they try to be more than what the world thinks they are.

Black Women who are tough and strong, who fight for their families and take the brunt of the violence the world throws.

Black Women who are sexual and in control, who have created and nurtured life and family on this continent for thousands of years.

Black Women whose love and laughter gives us light when the world is dark.

Blaque Showgirls is for the 'you've got an Aboriginal nose' and the 'you're so lucky you don't have your Dad's nose'.

For the 'Black bitch' 'Abo slut' and 'we don't have that shade of make up';

For the 'Are you sure you're Aboriginal' and the 'you're too light but I know you ain't white'.

For the 'you don't sound Black' and the 'can you Black it up?'

For the 'you're pretty for an Aboriginal' and the 'Aboriginal women look like apes'.

For the 'they all sniff petrol' and 'you're different from the other ones'.

For the 'Black sluts' and 'Black cunts'.

For the 'you all used to live in humpees' and the 'you wouldn't even be here if it wasn't for whites'.

For the skinny ankles and big bums and bigger hearts and bigger minds.

For Black Women who are magic because they are future.

Blaque Showgirls is for them. Because if this world ever changes for the better, it's because Black women pulled the fucking trigger!

NATHAN MAYNARD

The Season

The Season *takes us into the world of the mutton birding on the islands off Tasmania, where Aboriginal people have harvested the birds forever.*

In this scene, the matriarch of the family, Marlene, recounts her experience of being forced to 'prove' her Aboriginality to a bureaucrat.

Marlene

He might as well been talking German, because there was no way I was proving my Aboriginality to someone who woke up black 6 weeks ago.

But I got the little fuck, I bluffed. I had a power bill in this boob and a layby in the other, so I pulled the bill outta me top and me boob out with it. Well, you should have seen the poor little fuck's eyes, they popped out of his head that far, I thought they'd end up on his desk with me tit. So, now all straight-face like, I just left it sitting there. Well mate, he doesn't know where to look, but he's trying his hardest to keep his eyes on the bill.

And he's like, ah-um Miss, I think …' Well before he could finish, I say, 'Oh sorry matey, I've given you my power bill, my black certificate must be in my other boob.' And before I could take my other tit out, he goes, 'Nah it's all good Marlene.' Stamped a piece of paper and now 'wallah' I'm black again.

At What Cost?

This play focuses on the uniquely Tasmanian and contemporary experience whereby some people in Tasmania attempt to claim Aboriginal heritage, in order to put themselves in positions of influence and power, and the pushback from the Aboriginal community.

In this scene, Boyd talks to his deceased Uncle about the pain caused by these claimants.

Boyd wakes up from being knocked out.

These claimers are not part of this country's story.

They're not part of our story. They're not part of my story.

Beat. He shifts.

Where were they when I used to get called Abo at school?

Or when the teachers used to tell me I'm a half-caste.

Where were they when the cops used to bash me 'cause I'm 'Mansell scum'?

And where they when my nan used to break down talking about her dead sons who died locked up?

Tell me where they were when my uncle Colin was dragged out of bed, only to be found hours later swinging in his cell by his black neck.

And please tell me where they were after my sixteen-year-old cousin Lou Lou walked into the Launceston Trades Hotel, pulled a sawn-off shotgun out of her backpack, and blew her head off. Because the family sure coulda needed them then.

Where the fuck were they then, aye?

Had some book not told them they were black yet?

Had they not felt a connection yet?

Had the government not told them they were palawa yet?

[*Sadly*] And now my mob sit with them around our fire.

In this scene Boyd is bidding farewell to the remains of his deceased Uncle, William Lanne.

Boyd is left with Lanne's remains in his arms. They're inside the woven basket Nala made.

Ya Uncle.

Mina, trawlwoolway man Boyd Mansell, Laura and Athol's grandson, Tasman's boy. Our fellas have chosen me to build you the sky ladder, and send you up to the sky mob.

And what an honour they have given me.

This is the spot where you're gunna leave from.

See those rocks there, that's where we've sent other old coes before you up to the sky mob. When you're gone, you'll have your own rocks to mark where you left from.

I've been collecting nothing but the best dry limbs for you aye, get that sky ladder as hot as we can get it and get you up there to them ancestors as fast as we can.

BOYD *puts Lanne down and starts building the pyre.*

After all these years, you're going home Unc. Up where there's wallaby bounding about everywhere, abalone under every swaying piece of bull kelp, biggest crayfish under every hanging rock ledge, where's there's mutton birds in every burrow.

Every night will be a full moon and you'll dance and sing with them ancestors until you see that morning star hit the dawn sky.

You'll be young and strong again, and your family will be there waiting for you. Your mum, your dad won't let go of you. They'll cuddle and kiss you and smell the top of your head like you're a boy again.

And everyone will be waiting to see you William Lanne.

When them ancestors see you coming, their black faces will light up like the Milky Way.

You're not even in the sky yet but everyone knows you're a star.

One day when I get up there, I'd be tickled pink if I could dance and hunt with you and if you could show me the old ways. For you to introduce me to my old fellas. The thought of meeting chief Manalagenna.

I promise I'll get you there ole coe, I'll get you home to that sky mob, I swear on my unborn son's life I'll get you up to those ancestors.

And into your beautiful wife trukanini's waiting arms.

LEAH PURCELL

The Drover's Wife

Leah Purcell reimagines the classic short story The Drovers Wife, *by Henry Lawson, where a woman brings up her children in bush isolation while her husband is away. In her version a storyteller, a black man, turns up on her doorstep and she helps him out and they share stories. But neither of them are safe from the white men who seek to subjugate both the local Blacks and the women they find virtually defenceless. Molly must fight for her life.*

In this scene the Molly, awakening after being raped by the stockman McPharlen, spots the Aboriginal odd job man, Yadaka's, body hanging from a snow gum. She speaks of her son Danny.

Drover's Wife, speaking to dead Yadaka

love the snow gum. Its stout trunk strong … beautiful coloured patterns appear when wet; a gift from God. Sturdy tree's limbs waiting to take the weight of winter … the weight of you.

Oh, to see these snow gums after an autumn shower … it's this rare beauty that reminds me why I stay …

… a vision of beauty no more.

All I'll see now is you, pale face, neck broke … just an inch more and Joe's boot to the ground.

[*Singing*] Black, black, black is the colour of my true love's hair. Her face is something wondrous fair.

Black Mary.

My da, no mention of my ma's … name …

[*Singing*] The purest smile and the gentlest of hands …

Sang it when he was drunk …

    Beat.

Maybe that's why I'm a good tracker. Had the gift of findin' me da when he was on the drink.

Us always on our own … always away … or over there, never near or amongst, just … alone, just us, us two.

    Beat.

Miss Shirley McGuinness once said, 'Danny was quite brown … He might be a throwback?' Throwback, didn't know what that meant …

I told her I was workin' hard in the paddock … Danny still in my belly, 'He got some sun too …'

Maybe that's why Joe didn't like me when he was ragin' with the whiskey, beat me till I was black … and …

    Beat.

My da did once say …

Molly, pet name to Mary.

    Pause.

Black Mary. Whitest gin around.

DAVID MILROY

Windmill Baby

Set on an abandoned cattle station, Windmill Baby *is a poignant story like a campfire yarn. A single hander,* Windmill Baby *has multiple characters, including the mongrel camp dog, who weave their memories into a blanket of stories.*

In this concluding scene from the play, Old May is about to leave the station for the last time. She speaks to the deceased Ruby about her regrets at not having kept her promises to Ruby's daddy.

Old May

Ruby, I had to leave this station and there's a lot that I never got to tell you. Your daddy passed on now but I want you to know he was a good man and a good stockman and it was him that give you your name from that ruby stone. That ring is long gone. I know a lot of years have passed but I never stopped thinking about you and I've always loved you. [*Pause.*] Now, Wunman, I know you couldn't go to the mission and I know you couldn't stay on the station but when you left, a lot of goodness went with you… I want you to know that when that Windmill Baby came I also had nowhere to go. I had no choice either… I wish things could have been different. I'm sorry.

She takes a quilt from her bag and holds it.

The shadow of the windmill.

She stares at the windmill.

Windmill Baby, we never got across that river but I did my best. I haven't got much to give you now but here's that quilt me and your mummy made for you… I never got to keep my promise to your daddy… but maybe he come for you tonight… and he can tell you that story… you know that potato one. [*She puts the quilt down. Pause.*] How you end that story?

JADAH MILROY

Crow Fire

Crow Fire is a contemporary story centring on Dayna, a young urban First Nations woman who is working in government and frustrated with her inability to make a difference in the world. In a poetic and surreal gesture, she encounters Crow, a mystical force, and they try to influence a group of people in her orbit, including Tony, an activist, a politician and her disillusioned husband, and a young Aboriginal man who has come into the city from the desert.

In this scene, Dayna, who was raised white, talks about her anguish at having missed out on growing up with culture.

Dayna

No, Tony, you come on. It's easy for you, you may have lived on the mission but at least you had other Kooris around you. I have to fight every day—with who I am and who I want to be. I'll never have the chance to know what it's like to be brought up a blackfella, by blackfellas. My chance for that disappeared when they took my grandmother away. You think I don't wish I could just go bush, wave a magic wand and esto presto instant culture? Culture has to be lived, it has to be learnt through experience over time—it comes from the land itself! You can't take a crash course during your midyear holiday.

Beat.

I was raised white, Tony—in a white society, with a white education, white family and white friends. The only thing black about me is the little bit of DNA in this finger, [*sticking up a rude finger*] my relationship to Crow and a spirit that loves this land and hates this bullshit mono-culture called 'mainstream Australia'. The most I can hope for right now is to help preserve what cultural heartlands are left and try to repair some of the damage.

TRACEY RIGNEY

Belonging

Belonging *tells the tale of Cindy, 13 and a schoolgirl, who is struggling with her sense of identity and belonging in the small river town where she lives. A series of life-changing events occurs and she is drawn into to the drug-fuelled life of her cousin Janice, only 14 but tough and hardened.*

In this scene, Cindy is wrestling with the mistakes she has made, as she talks to her father, who has passed away.

Cindy

Dad? [*Pause.*] It's me. Cindy. [*Pause.*] I feel terrible, Dad. [*Pause.*] Terrible about the stupid things I've done. [*Upset*] I'm such a fuck up, Dad! I don't know what I'm doing with myself. I hate myself. [*Pause.*] But I hate myself even more now for hurting those I love.

Silence.

[*Upset, quietly*] You're probably turning in your grave now because of me.

Silence as CINDY *composes herself.*

It's like… there's a war inside. [*Pause.*] My head, fighting my heart. [*Pause.*] But in this war—there are no winners. [*Pause.*] Just all losers.

Silence. She becomes a little thoughtful.

You know, every birthday, when I close my eyes and blow out my candles to make a wish, I always wish… for you to be here… with me and Mum. [*Pause.*] And when I open my eyes, all I see is the smoke from the candles. I still cling onto my wish, hoping that when the smoke clears, you'll appear from behind it. [*Pause.*] But you don't. [*Pause.*] You can't.

Silence.

But deep down inside… [*Pause*] I somehow know you're with us. [*Pause.*] You're always with us. [*Pause.*] I know you're here right now. Listening. [*Pause.*] And I know that I have to undo—what I've done. [*Pause.*] Because that's what you would do. [*Pause.*] Wouldn't you? [*Pause.*] So I guess it's up to me.

DANIEL RILEY, AMY SOLE, URSULA YOVICH

Tracker

In Tracker, *a powerful story is told of Alec 'Tracker' Riley, who served in the New South Wales Police Force for 40 years, using his deep cultural knowledge in leading high-profile searches for missing people and becoming a legend in the force. Alec balanced life as a Wiradjuri man and as a tracker in a colonial system that worked against Aboriginal people.*

In this scene, Alec describes his connection to place.

Alec

Been here over fifty years now. Me and Ethel. Raised the kids here. [*Beat.*] It's a big reserve, 18 acres … [*Beat.*] Four families here … around thirty three people at the moment. The Taylors, the Burns family over there, in the old teacher's cottage it's me and Ethel and over through that scrub is the Carrs. Been here since the beginning. Some of the folks have moved on … Dubbo, Sydney … Things change …

Beat.

I'm not moving to Dubbo.

I am most happy out here … I get my water from the rivers, always have ... I like the exercise, keeps me fit. Got the kerosene lamps, the ice box ... We hunt our own food. Help each other out, watch each other's kids. We know each and every family here. We've grown old ... together. Our celebrations and ceremonies ... It's all wrapped up in this place. And now they want us to move along. Move us on to bigger and better ...

Beat.

Got this watch after forty years service. No pension just a watch, A timepiece ... but it can not measure forty years. You can't measure the sum of my life ... And what about the time before Gabaa Gibir.

Beat.

This was my home. It still is ... It's been our land for a long time. You know that and I know that ...

This country is not mine to give or yours to take ... but it's where I belong, where my children belong and their children and their children's children ... we are imbued with her spirit, from the roots up. I sit outside your circle not because you won't let me in ... but being inside that circle means to give up the old ways. To give up my deep connection. We will never do that. We belong here.

MARYANNE SAM

Casting Doubts

Casting Doubts *takes us into the world of the casting agency and deals with the issue of racism within the industry and how it manifests, including 'authenticity' around the fraught idea of the perfect Blak actor.*

In this scene, Linda, an actress, has to deal with stereotypical roles as the Aboriginal 'victim'.

Linda

know it's work. I've done it before. But it's getting to me, Mick. More and more. It's getting to me. *Corroboree Dreaming*, right? Well, they've given me this shapeless white costume that I have to rub in the gutter to dirty myself up with... I'm constantly manhandled during rehearsals and performance, not to mention the fact that I think my co-star is starting to enjoy the assault scenes... I've had my lines cut because the director doesn't think a respectful Aboriginal woman would talk like that... but he's certainly happy for me to talk like 'dis'...! They've got me reciting some mumbo jumbo that I don't think exists... I've got more spiritual moments than I know what to do with and they all look at me nodding knowingly, like I'm some guru who has the answers to the world's problems! And they smile at me, Mick. They're always smiling at me... I'm not an actor to them. I'm just an Aborigine. And I'm sick of it!

In this scene Jimi riffs on the lack of opportunities he faces as a Blak actor, despite his training and experience.

Jimi [*voiceover*]

And who's behind door number three? It's Jimi Jackson. Jimi's a professional actor. Studied three years at the Performing Arts Academy. You might have seen some of his work as long as you didn't blink. You could say he's pretty particular about the roles he takes. Jimi is a consultant to the blacktracker fraternity and linguists have marvelled at his grasp of language: 'Yes, boss, no boss, three bags full boss.' C'mon out and tell us a bit more about yourself, Jimi!

JIMI: Bloody doors. Opening. Closing. Slamming. Shutting. Creaking—doors. Knocked on a few in my time. Actually got in the front door, for a few seconds, only to find it was a revolving door. Sorry, no time. Sorry, no thank you. Not interested. Not today. Don't come pedalling your wares. Hawkers beware. Jehovah is your witness.

Witness? What will we witness behind closed doors? Today we have black men. Black men who will sing and dance if you throw coins at their feet. Black men who will don a mask other than their own to atone—for... whose sins...?

Comfortable chairs. Relaxed and comfortable atmosphere.

Comforting glances. Just be comfortable in your own skin. Cold comfort when you've got to uphold *their* lies and furnish *their* comfort zones. I'm one such black man who has sung and danced for thirty pieces of silver. But no more. Cause once I get my foot in the door, fuckin' watch out!

KIRLI SAUNDERS

Going Home

Jedda's mum Luina was raised off-Country as a state ward in a children's home after being forcibly removed from her family. Jedda has inherited the disconnection and displacement many First Nations Peoples experience as a result. His sister, Arkie, is a queer solo mum-to-be who is trying to encourage him to go home and reconnect to Country and community. In this monologue, Jedda sits with the complexities of being raised off-Country, being a Dad and his hesitancy to confront the intergenerational traumas which are present in his day-to-day life in the city.

Jedda

Takes a cleva spirit to sing up a loved one,
our son can do it– Little Monti.
He be there, smiling and laughing at an Ancestor in the corner,
worrying all our white friends 'hey man, who's your kid talking to?'
Alani and I try to convince them he's not possessed
He's always conspiring with the Old People–
Can Sing in Nan Emmie–
she was his first word.
He made me realise I can see them, can hear them too,
But I try not to let it be known. Feels like magic I shouldn't be

touching with these hands

You know, I've only been back for sorry business once with Mum and Dad

Only ever gone home to grieve.

I never learnt to dance with my cousins and the Old fullas,

can't utter a word in Nan's language,

When they ask me at work about yidaki and ceremony

and I don't know what to say,

I can play, sure, but those ancient song lines aren't awake in me

I'm always the joker in the centre making the long lunch break shorter for the apprentice, see, I don't want little cuz being called what they name me

I'm tired of calling it out and white fragility.

I hide away up here in the city where I can handle the racist slurs,

where kids on their Ps call me the 'N' word, and I be there trying to not throw my large taro milk tea, no sugar, half ice at them.

Same city where people hide their purse when I walk by, as if our land wasn't enough, they gotta keep the clutch close too.

Same city where they assume I'm unemployed when I have a day off with my baby boy.

I've been toying with Arkie's invite to go home.

But how do I tell her I got too much work on

that Alani needs me

I can't bear to go to a place where I'm from,

but am not known

can't go showing up unannounced.

I don't think they'd even recognise me—

Family down there.

I got my family here to worry about,

Wanna get life set up for Monti.

In all honesty, here, there
I'm not sure where I belong.

Monti cries on the monitor.
I hear you crying my boy,
I'm coming little one.

URSULA YOVICH AND ALANA VALENTINE

Barbara and the Camp Dogs

Wild and unpredictable, Barbara and her sister Rene front a pub band and rock out everything from mournful ballads to rock to punk-inspired tunes. But their mother is dying back home, and they need to return to country and face their demons, including finding Barbara's long-separated brother, before it's too late.

In this scene, Barbara spews out the rage she feels about everything in her life going wrong, and how she blames herself.

Barbara

I storm out. I run like a fire out of control consuming everything in its path, ready to swing, lash out. I'm not running because I'm pissed at René, I'm running because that's what I'm good at. I run and I run and the next thing I know I'm standing outside the Stuart Hotel. I need to forget. I'm skint and I need to fucking forget. I see some countrymen sitting on the median strip. Drinking. I go to them. 'Hey, Aunty … Unc.' 'Where you from, my girl, who your family?' this old girl asks. 'I'm from here.' I tell 'em, 'Mum's in hospital. Dying.' And they cry, just like that, they cry 'cause they know. They just know. I sit down and they pass me the cask and I'm drinking hard. Listening hard. All night I listen to stories, drunken, fighting stories, mixed in with the good old days! Kids and country and youth and dreams and everything every other fucker in this fucked-up town talks about. The good shit gone bad! And then I'm yelling, 'They dumped me like rubbish! Like fucking rubbish!' I fall asleep. Drunk.

I have this nightmare where I look down between my legs and I see this blood pouring out and then I look in my hand and there's my dick, the dick that I never had, and I run after my dad and my brother calling to them that I've got a dick, I really do have one, and then I trip, and I'm crying, pleading with them to wait for me.

I feel the boot. Police. Someone's screaming? It's the old girl. She's stripped down to her skirt, her breast exposed, and she's thumping at her chest … 'You fucking take everything! I know you, you fuckin' shit! I know you. It's you mob, took my kids. You got kids?! Huh?! You fuckin' fuck!' The officer laughs. 'You want your kids, then clean up your act.' He's rough. He lifts her skinny body off the ground and shoves her into the back of the paddy wagon and she goes quiet. Knocked out. I manage to get up and I'm spewing hatred at this man. He says, 'You're going into the lockup as well'. I try to run but my legs are useless and I fall to the ground. I got to get to the hospital, I say, 'Please, I gotta get to the hospital'. He looks at me with disgust and shoves me in the back with the old girl. 'Not tonight you're not.'

And I'm in the back of the paddy wagon thinking. I went and fucked up again. So I'm kicking at the walls and screaming at them. They brake hard so I slide across the floor and hit my head on the steel seats. My head spins. But I'm angry. 'You're all sick.' They slam the brakes again and this time I feel my shoulder bruise up. I'm crying. 'Please. Please. I need to see my mum …'

She screams.

You hate us 'cause we're black or pity us 'cause we're black. Which is worse? You whitefellas have an infection that makes you think that I really am different. Shit, you get crazy with hatred or crazy with guilt, one minute we're more real and the next we're primitive natives. This is the meanest, pettiest, most ungenerous country in the world.

Because at the heart of this country is a theft, and now the whole place crouches, waiting, calculating about when it is going to be stolen back from them. Because nobody fears being thieved from as much as a pack of thieves, a gang, a group. A nation. And I understand theft. Of community, of culture, of language, of family. Belonging. I wanted to belong somewhere, and I never belonged here. And I think of Mum Tanya, of my dad, of my brother Joseph. I mostly think of Mum Jill in that hospital, waiting, thinking I don't care.

In this scene Barbara describes her trip on a motorbike as she races toward her brother.

Barbara

I get on the bike and I drive. Dust flying at me, getting in my eyes and nose and ears. It's a straight line from Katherine to Bulman. One road in, one road out. I'm speeding. Speeding down this dirt road, and I feel the tyres lift every time I hit a patch of soft dirt. I can't slow down. I can't 'cause it doesn't matter and I don't care. My feet stay firm on the accelerator. The sun is in my eyes. And I remember Mum sitting on the bed with the halo of light around her ...

I can't see now 'cause the tears won't stop. I pull over and I've made it to Flying Fox Creek. The creek is shallow and clear, I can see the white sand and the flecks of gold and brown pebbles ... The massive paperbark trees stand guard, lining the bank, giving shade ... And I remember him ... Joseph. My little brother. And I see him. His crooked teeth showing through his big smile, and René is there too, and me. I'm making this makeshift canoe out of paperbark and sticks and they're arguing over who gets to ride it down the river first ... I remember this day. I say, 'I'll make it bigger so you can both go on it first, just stop fighting' ... They jump on me. Hugging me. Now they're arguing again. 'She's my sister' ... 'No! She's my sister!'

The sound of Bulman at night.

I'd been telling myself that it was going to be really hard to find him and where would I start to look, but I go out there and it's easy. I ask these snotty-nosed kids at the tuckshop. They know who he is. They point me to where he's living. Too easy. Shamefully easy. I've told myself that he's so far away and it turns out that he was just there and all it took was me to make the move. And that's when I realise how bad I've fucked up with Mum, you know. Because even though she's gone, she's still teaching me. She's still showing me that the way you live is to put your arm out, not wait for the other person to always put theirs out first. You offer the love and that's how you get it back. And now she's gone and I'm too late. I'm too late. And that's me, you know, that's me. I always work it out when everyone around me has just had a-fuckin-nuff of trying to reach for me and coming up with a handful of nothing. 'Cause that's what I am, that's what I'll always be. Just a handful of nothing worth anything. And I'm too late for Mum to know that I know she tried, I know she loved me. But maybe she's looking down and maybe if I reach out my hand to Joseph, maybe she'll know that I've finally worked it out. And then I'm there. I'm standing in front of him.

ABOUT THE AUTHORS

JANE HARRISON is descended from the Muruwari people of NSW. Her first play *Stolen* had productions across Australia and toured internationally. Other works include *Rainbow's End*, *The Visitors*, and the novel *Becoming Kirrali Lewis*, which was shortlisted for the Prime Minister's Literary Awards and the Victorian Premier's Literary Awards. Both *Stolen* and *Rainbow's End* have been placed on secondary school curricula. Jane is the Festival Director of Blak & Bright First Nations Literary Festival (2016, 2019, 2022).

JADA ALBERTS is a Larrakia, Bardi, Wadaman and Yanuwa actor/director/writer from the Top End of Australia. Writing credits include: TV series *Cleverman*, the play *Brothers Wreck*; acting credits include: *Cleverman*, *Rush*, *Redfern Now*, *Wentworth*; directing credits include *Aretha* Australian Tour, *The 7 Stages of Grieving* for Browns Mart Theatre and the 2018 tour of Jada's critically acclaimed play *Brothers Wreck*. In 2014 Jada won the Balnaves Foundation Indigenous Playwrights Award and *Brothers Wreck* received nominations for the 2014 Sydney Theatre Awards for Best New Australian Work, Best Stage Play at the 2015 AWGIE Awards and made the shortlist for the Nick Enright Prize for Playwriting at the 2015 NSW Premier's Literary Awards.

HENRIETTA BAIRD is from the Kuku Yalanji people in Far North Queensland. A graduate of NAISDA Dance Association, Henrietta has performed in many notable productions across

Australia and internationally, including *My Right Foot Your Right Foot*, *Pop Whistle Crack*, *Stolen*, *The Stirring*, *Dancing Smoke* and *Divercity*. In 2017 Henrietta part of the Yellamundie festival, writing her first playscript *The Weekend*. Works in development include *Hacking the Anthropacine*, *Plant a Promise* and the dance work, *Song Spirals*. When not performing, Henrietta is part of the Indigenous Education team at Royal Botanic Gardens where she leads tours and creates educational programs learning about native bush plants and the history of the Sydney people.

KODIE BEDFORD was born in Geraldton, Western Australia, with strong family ties to East Kimberley. Kodie's television drama credits include *Mystery Road* (ABC), *Summer Love* (ABC), *Firebite* (AMC+) and *All My Friends are Racist* (ABC). Kodie received Belvoir's Balnaves Fellowship in 2019 and her play *Cursed!* was staged in 2020, winning best stage play and the major award at the 2021 Australian Writers' Guild Awards. At home Kodie likes to drink copious amounts of tea, catch up on royal family news and spend time helping foster dogs in need of a new home.

WESLEY ENOCH has written and directed iconic Indigenous productions *The 7 Stages of Grieving*, *Black Medea* and *The Story of the Miracle at Cookie's Table*. He has directed productions of *The Sapphires*, *Black Diggers*, *I am Eora*, *Yibiyung*, *Parramatta Girls*, *Raisin in the Sun* and *Appropriate*. He was the Artistic Director of the Sydney Festival from 2017 to 2020. Wesley's other residencies include Resident Director at Sydney Theatre Company; Associate Artistic Director at Belvoir Street Theatre; the 2002 Australia Council Cite Internationale des Arts Residency in Paris and the Australia Council Artistic Director for the Australian Delegation to the 2008 Festival of Pacific Arts. He was creative consultant, segment director and indigenous consultant for the 2018 Gold Coast Commonwealth Games and the QUT Indigenous Chair of Creative Industries.

RICHARD FRANKLAND is an Aboriginal Australian of Gunditjmara origin from Victoria. In 1993 Richard co-wrote and directed the documentary *Songlines*. His wide range of video, documentary and film projects include the award-winning *Who Killed Malcolm Smith*, *No Way To Forget*, *After Mabo*, *Harry's War* and *Stone Bros*. Richard's plays include *Conversations with the Dead*, *Walking into the Bigness* and *An Evening with Richard Frankland*. Frankland founded the Mirimbiak Nations Aboriginal Corporation and was instrumental in forming Australians for Native Title and Reconciliation (ANTAR), and the Your Voice political party after the abolition of ATSIC.

DR ANITA HEISS is an award-winning author of non-fiction, historical fiction, commercial women's fiction and children's novels. She is a proud member of the Wiradyuri Nation of central New South Wales, an Ambassador for the Indigenous Literacy Foundation and the GO Foundation. Anita is a board member of the National Justice Project and Circa Contemporary Circus. She is Professor of Communications at the University of Queensland, and as an artist in residence at La Boite Theatre adapted her novel *Tiddas* for the stage.

ANDREA JAMES is a Yorta Yorta/Gunaikurnai theatremaker and graduate of VCA. Her plays include *Yanagai! Yanagai!*, which toured to the UK, *Winyanboga Yurringa*, *Sunshine Super Girl*, which had an extensive national tour and was nominated for four Green Room awards, and *Dogged* (with Catherine Ryan). Andrea is Associate Artistic Director at Griffin Theatre where directing credits include *Ghosting the Party* and *Jailbaby*. In 2022 Andrea received the Mona Brand Award for Women Stage and Screen Writers, Australia's most prestigious writing prize for women.

NAKKIAH LUI is a writer and Gamillaroi and Torres Strait Islander woman. Her plays include *This Heaven*; *I Should Have Told You Before We Made Love (That I'm Black)*; *Blackie Blackie Brown: The Traditional Owners of Death*; *Kill the Messenger*; *Power Plays*; *Black is the New White*;

Blak Cabaret, *How to Rule the World* and *Blaque Showgirls*. For TV and film she has written *Black Comedy* (in which she also appeared); *Kiki and Kitty*, *Get Krack!n*, *Preppers*, *From Drag King to Law Queen*, and *BabyGirl*. Nakkiah has received many awards including the Balnaves Award and Malcolm Robertson Prize, and has been a contributor to *The Guardian*, *The Drum* and *Q&A*, among others.

NATHAN MAYNARD is a Trawlwoolway, pakana man and actor, writer and director from Lutruwita/Tasmania. Nathan's plays include *The Season*, *At What Cost?* and *Hide the Dog* (with Jamie Mc Caskill). He has written, produced and directed for animation series *Little J & Big Cuz* (in palawa kani, a Tasmanian Aboriginal language), and *Zero Point*. He was co-creator, dramaturg and director of Naz Dickenson's debut play *CRUMBS*, and acted in the TV show *Deadloch*. Nathan received the Tasmanian Aboriginal Artist of the Year Award in 2006 and 2013, and the Tasmania Aboriginal of the Year Award in 2018.

LEAH PURCELL is a proud Goa-Gunggari-Wakka Wakka Murri woman from Queensland. She is an actor, writer and director who has appeared in and directed numerous theatre, film and TV productions, including *Radiance*, *Brothers Wreck*, *Parramatta Girls*, *Cleverman*, *Wentworth*, *Redfern Now*, *Last Cab to Darwin*, and many more. She wrote and acted in her play *The Drover's Wife*, which she also turned into a film and novel, and *Box the Pony* (with Scott Rankin). Her many awards include AACTA, Helpmann, Matilada, and Film Critics' Circle awards, and the prestigious Eisenhower Fellowship.

DAVID MILROY is a Palyku man whose country is in the Pilbara. David was the first Artistic Director of Yirra Yaakin Aboriginal Theatre and in 2002 received a Myer Award for his contribution to the development of indigenous theatre. David received the 2004 Patrick White Award and the 2005 Equity Guild Award for his play *Windmill Baby*. David was also a finalist in the Helpmann Awards and received two Equity Guild Awards in 2011 for his play *Waltzing* *the Wilarra*. David has had a number of works commissioned and presented at WAAPA. David most recent work was *Panawathi Girl* in the 2022 Perth International Arts Festival.

JADAH MILROY, a Victorian College of the Arts and Aboriginal Centre for the Performing Arts graduate, is a proud Palku woman, who has worked as an artistic director, actor, playwright, dramaturge, animateur, director, tutor and event coordinator. Her plays include *Jidja*, musical drama *The Promise*, cross discipline Journey to Adolescence, The Sand Crab, Touch the Air and Crow Fire. Crow Fire was shortlisted for the Malcolm Robertson Prize 2002, the Kate Challis Raka Award 2002 and the NSW Premier's Literary Award 2003. Milroy was an International Ensemble Member of 'Full Circle' Native Performance Company in Vancouver, Canada and is an experienced ensemble trainer in theatremaking.

TRACEY RIGNEY got her love of storytelling from her Grandfather and family. A Wotjobaluk and Ngarrindjeri woman, she draws inspiration from her people and culture. She began her career in the theatre as a playwright with her debut play *Belonging*. She went on to write a couple of more plays before transitioning to film and TV and has written and directed a number of short films before contributing to the feature film, *We are still here* 2022. The same year she wrote both Windmill Theatre's stage play *Rella* and a children's play, *Someone In the Dark* for Black Hole Theatre.

MARYANNE SAM completed her Masters in Writing for Performance at VCA, Melbourne University 2019. A founding member of Ilbijerri Theatre Company, Maryanne's credits include *Oh My God I'm Blak*, Yirramboi 2023 (Director/Producer/CoDevisor) *The Whisper* by Brodie Murray Melbourne Fringe Festival 2022 (Director), *Coconut Woman* Yirramboi 2021, (Writer/Director/Producer) *Viral* Ilbijerri Theatre (Writer) *Coconut Woman* Readings (Blak and Bright Festival 2019, Ballarat Art Gallery 2018, Malthouse

Jan 2018, Yellamundie Festival, Sydney, 2017) and more. Maryanne is recipient of the inaugural Ilbijerri Theatre's Uncle Bob Maza Award for 'Outstanding Contribution to Victorian Theatre', the Centenary Medal for 'Services to Indigenous Arts' and the Australia Council for The Arts, ATSI Arts Board Fellowship.

KIRLI SAUNDERS (OAM) is a proud Gunai Woman and award-winning author, multidisciplinary artist and consultant. An experienced speaker and facilitator advocating for the environment and equality, Kirli was the NSW Aboriginal Woman of the Year (2020). In 2022, she was awarded an Order of Australia Medal for her contribution to the arts, particularly literature. Kirli has partnered with global organisations including Google, Fender, Sydney Opera House, Qantas and Spotify, Mecca and Aesop to celebrate stories and cultivate change. Her celebrated books among others include *Bindi*, *Our Dreaming*, *Kindred*, and *Returning* (Magabala Books). Her play, *Going Home*, will take the stage in 2024. She is also writing her anticipated novel, *Yaraman* assisted by the Australia Council.

URSULA YOVICH grew up in the Northern Territory, in Darwin and Maningrida. She has appeared at venues including the Queen Elizabeth Hall in London, Carnegie Hall in New York, and the Concert Hall at the Sydney Opera House. Yovich won the Balnaves Foundation Indigenous Playwright's Award in 2016. Acting credits include *Diving for Pearls*, *Heart is a Wasteland*, *Love and Information*, *Mother Courage and Her Children*, *Barefoot Divas*, *Waltzing the Wilarra*, the national tour of the one-woman show *The Magic Hour*, and her cabaret show *Magpie Blues*, which had its world premiere in Adelaide and toured major venues across Australia. Yovich has been nominated for Helpmann Awards for her performances in *Mother Courage and Her Children* and *Magpie Blues*.

ALANA VALENTINE is a multi-award-winning playwright, director, and librettist. Her play *Wayside Bride* played at Belvoir in

2022. Having worked with Bangarra Dance Theatre for ten years as dramaturg, in 2022 Alana was the co-writer, with Stephen Page, of *Wudjang: Not the Past*, music by Steve Francis. At the 2022 Adelaide Festival Alana was the co-librettist, with Christos Tsiolkas, of *Watershed: The Death of Dr Duncan*, music by Joe Twist, directed by Neil Armfield. Her plays are published by Currency Press, including a book about her verbatim/close work practice, *Bowerbird: The art of making theatre drawn from life*.

SOURCES

Alberts, J. (2014). *Brothers Wreck*. Currency Press, pp. 38–3. Copyright © Jada Alberts. Reproduced with the permission of the author.

Baird, H. (2019). *The Weekend*. Supplied by the author, pp. 23–4, 40. Copyright © Henrietta Baird. Reproduced with the permission of the author.

Bedford, K. (2022). *Cursed*. Currency Press, pp. 1–2. Copyright © Lovely B Pictures Pty Ltd. Reproduced with the permission of the author.

Enoch, W. (2007). *Black Medea*, published in *Contemporary Indigenous Plays*. Currency Press, p. 61. Copyright © Wesley Enoch. Reproduced with the permission of the author.

Enoch, W. (2007). *The Story of the Miracle at Cookie's Table*. Currency Press, pp. 11, 26. Copyright © Wesley Enoch. Reproduced with the permission of the author.

Frankland, R. (2002). *Conversations with the Dead*, published in *Blak Inside*. Currency Press, p. 229. Copyright © Richard J Frankland. Reproduced with the permission of the author.

Frankland, R. (2017). *Walking into the Bigness*. Currency Press, pp. 19–20, 10. Copyright © Richard J Frankland. Reproduced with the permission of the author.

Harrison, J. (2014). *Stolen*. Currency Press, pp. 22–3. Copyright © Jane Harrison. Reproduced with the permission of the author.

Harrison, J. (2007). *Rainbow's End*, published in *Contemporary Indigenous Plays*. Currency Press, p. 196–8. Copyright © Jane Harrison. Reproduced with the permission of the author.

Harrison, J. (2021). *The Visitors*. Currency Press, p. 50. Copyright © Jane Harrison. Reproduced with the permission of the author.

Heiss, A. (2022). *Tiddas*. Playlab Theatre, p. 59. Copyright © Anita Heiss. Reproduced with the permission of the author and the publisher.

James, A. (2019). *Winyanboga Yurringa*. Currency Press, p. 30–1. Copyright © Andrea James. Reproduced with the permission of the author.

James, A. (2016). *Yanagai! Yanagai!* (revised edition) Currency Press, p. 51. Copyright © Andrea James. Reproduced with the permission of the author.

James, A. (2021). *Sunshine Super Girl.* Currency Press, p. 1–2. Copyright © Andrea James. Reproduced with the permission of the author.

James, A. (2021). *Dogged.* Currency Press, p. 12–14. Copyright © Andrea James and Catherine Ryan. Reproduced with the permission of the authors.

Lui, N. (2019). *Black is the New White.* Allen and Unwin. Copyright © Nakkiah Lui. Reproduced with the permission of the author and publisher.

Lui, N. (2023). *Blaque Showgirls.* Currency Press, pp. 25–6, 50–1. Copyright © Nakkiah Lui. Reproduced with the permission of the author.

Maynard, N. (2018). *The Season.* Supplied by the author. Copyright © Nathan Maynard. Reproduced with the permission of the author.

Maynard, N. (2023). *At What Cost.* Currency Press, pp. 47, 21–2. Copyright © Nathan Maynard. Reproduced with the permission of the author.

Purcell, L. (2017). *The Drover's Wife.* Currency Press, pp. 53–4. Copyright © Leah Purcell. Reproduced with the permission of the author.

Milroy, D. (2007). *Windmill Baby*, published in *Contemporary Indigenous Plays.* Currency Press, pp. 227. Copyright © David Milroy. Reproduced with the permission of the author.

Milroy, J. (2002). *Crow Fire*, published in *Blak Inside.* Currency Press, p. 182. Copyright © Jadah Milroy. Reproduced with the permission of the author.

Rigney, T. (2002). *Belonging*, published in *Blak Inside.* Currency Press, pp. 102–3. Copyright © Tracey Rigney. Reproduced with the permission of the author.

Riley, D., A. Sole, and U. Yovich. (2023). *Tracker.* Supplied by the authors. Copyright © Daniel Riley, Amy Sole and Ursula Yovich. Reproduced with the permission of the authors.

Sam, M. (2001). *Casting Doubts*, published in *Blak Inside.* Currency Press, pp. 130, 143. Copyright © Maryanne Sam. Reproduced with the permission of the author.

Saunders, K. (nd). *Going Home.* Supplied by the author. Copyright © Kirli Saunders. Reproduced with the permission of the author.

Yovich, U and A. Valentine (2017). *Barbara and the Camp Dogs.* Currency Press, pp. 34–5, 38–9. Copyright © Ursula Yovich and Alana Valentine. Reproduced with the permission of the authors.

www.ingramcontent.com/pod-product-compliance
Lightning Source LLC
Chambersburg PA
CBHW050023090426
42734CB00021B/3386